This Journal Belongs To:

_____

Introduction....

Journaling is a fun and creative way to document your life, get your thoughts and feelings out, and create a portrait of your inner most thoughts during the present time. No matter your age, journaling not only helps you better understand the present, but it also acts as a time capsule for you to revisit over and over as you get older.

Everyone can benefit from journaling, but some people are unsure what to write when staring at a blank page. That's where prompts come in. Prompts give you little ideas to help get you started, and the weekly calendar encourages you to write a small amount on your own each day.

This Journal gives you weekly prompts that promote self exploration, goal planning, positive thinking, list making, creative writing, imaginative thinking, and more. You are encouraged to grab your favorite pack of color pens and write, draw, color and doodle all over this book to make it uniquely your own.

MONDAY __/__/__

TUESDAY __/__/__

WEDNESDAY __/__/__

THURSDAY __/__/__

FRIDAY __/__/__

SATURDAY __/__/__

SUNDAY __/__/__

WEEK 1

☆ This is the first week of a whole year with this book. Write about one *goal* you would like to achieve before the book ends.

_____

☆ What *steps* do you need to take to get there?

_____

_____

_____

_____

☆ When will you get *started*? _____

☆ How will you *feel* when it's done? _____

_____

_____

_____

WEEK 2

☆ Everyone has *beauty* of their own, something that is unique to them, something only they have. Remember that beauty is not just on the outside but on the inside too, in the kindness hidden within you. Take a selfie this week, make sure your picture shows the inner you as well as the outer you. This is who you are today, in this moment. Print it and attach it to this page and write 3 things you love about yourself, inside or out.

MONDAY __/__/__

TUESDAY __/__/__

WEDNESDAY __/__/__

THURSDAY __/__/__

FRIDAY __/__/__

SATURDAY __/__/__

SUNDAY __/__/__

MONDAY __/__/__

TUESDAY __/__/__

WEDNESDAY __/__/__

THURSDAY __/__/__

FRIDAY __/__/__

SATURDAY __/__/__

SUNDAY __/__/__

WEEK 3

☆ Describe your *family*.

☆ How many people are in your family and what are their names? _____

_____

☆ Who's the oldest? _____

☆ Who's the youngest? _____

☆ Who's the smartest? _____

☆ Who's the funniest? _____

☆ Who are you most like? _____

☆ Who is the weirdest? _____

☆ When you grow up do you want to have a family of your own? On a sheet of paper, write about the future family you envision. How many kids, their names, where you will live, etc. When you are done, carefully fold the paper and tuck it between these pages for safe keeping.

WEEK 4

☆ If you could travel anywhere in the **world** right now, where would you go and why?

_____

_____

☆ Write about your journey and list 5 things you would do on your adventure. Create your very own magic ticket, and tuck it in this page for safe keeping.

_____

_____

_____

_____

_____

_____

_____

_____

MONDAY __/__/__

TUESDAY __/__/__

WEDNESDAY __/__/__

THURSDAY __/__/__

FRIDAY __/__/__

SATURDAY __/__/__

SUNDAY __/__/__

Journal or Schedule Important Moments from your Week

MONDAY __/__/__

TUESDAY __/__/__

WEDNESDAY __/__/__

THURSDAY __/__/__

FRIDAY __/__/__

SATURDAY __/__/__

SUNDAY __/__/__

WEEK 5

☆Describe your *friends*

☆ Who are your best friends?

☆ What do you love about them?

☆ What do you have most in common with them?

☆ What makes you unique from them?

☆ What do you love to do with them?

☆ Describe how you met them.

WEEK 6

☆ Lets play Would You Rather. Circle the one you choose.

- Would you rather eat a whole lemon or raw potato?

- Would you rather have robot daddy or a space alien mom?

- Would you rather explore the bottom of the ocean or another planet?

- Would you rather have the ability to turn invisible, or the ability to freeze time?

- Would you rather have all the snacks you ever want, or all the toys?

- Would you rather live in a place that rains every day, or a place that never rains?

- Would you rather travel every day or never leave home forever?

- Would you rather be able to play every musical instrument, or speak every language?

- Would you rather have the ability to smell colors, or see smells?

- Would you rather stand in a barrel of snakes, or lay in a nest of spiders?

- Would you rather live in a tree house or an underground house?

- Would you rather be able to draw perfectly, or sing perfectly?

- Would you rather be as tiny as a bug or as big as a giant dinosaur?

- Would you rather have 2 noses, or 1 eye?

Journal or Schedule Important Moments from your Week

MONDAY __/__/__

TUESDAY __/__/__

WEDNESDAY __/__/__

THURSDAY __/__/__

FRIDAY __/__/__

SATURDAY __/__/__

SUNDAY __/__/__

MONDAY __/__/__

TUESDAY __/__/__

WEDNESDAY __/__/__

THURSDAY __/__/__

FRIDAY __/__/__

SATURDAY __/__/__

SUNDAY __/__/__

WEEK 7

☆ List 10 things you want to accomplish *before* you are an adult. Be as creative as you want with your list. Don't be afraid to *dream big*.

_____

_____

_____

_____

_____

_____

_____

_____

_____

WEEK 8

☆ Some people are great at keeping secrets, others...not so much.
Which are you and why do you think that is?

_____

_____

_____

_____

_____

_____

_____

_____

_____

Journal or Schedule Important Moments from your Week

MONDAY __/__/__

TUESDAY __/__/__

WEDNESDAY __/__/__

THURSDAY __/__/__

FRIDAY __/__/__

SATURDAY __/__/__

SUNDAY __/__/__

MONDAY __/__/__

TUESDAY __/__/__

WEDNESDAY __/__/__

THURSDAY __/__/__

FRIDAY __/__/__

SATURDAY __/__/__

SUNDAY __/__/__

WEEK 9

☆ If you could have any animal as a pet, what would it be?

☆ What would you name it?

☆ What tricks would you teach it?

☆ Where would you keep it?

☆ What would you feed it?

☆ What would make owning this pet a unique experience?

WEEK 10

☆ Do you ever wish you could design your own animal? Draw a animal of your creation into existence. It can be big or small, have scales or fur, can have any color, even rainbow dots, can have wings or fins, and any special ability you can think of, the choice is yours.

MONDAY __/__/__

TUESDAY __/__/__

WEDNESDAY __/__/__

THURSDAY __/__/__

FRIDAY __/__/__

SATURDAY __/__/__

SUNDAY __/__/__

MONDAY __/__/__

TUESDAY __/__/__

WEDNESDAY __/__/__

THURSDAY __/__/__

FRIDAY __/__/__

SATURDAY __/__/__

SUNDAY __/__/__

☆ Mistakes are *learning experiences* that we all go through no matter what age we are. No one wants to make a mistake, but when we do, we usually grow from our experience and become better. Write about a mistake you've made in the past.

☆ Did you manage to fix your mistake?

☆ Will you ever make that mistake again?

☆ What did you learn from your experience?

WEEK 12

☆ Describe your 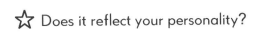. What kind of things can be found in it?

☆ How does it make you feel?

☆ Does it reflect your personality?

☆ What's your favorite thing in your room?

☆ If you could change one thing about your room, what would it be?

MONDAY __/__/__

TUESDAY __/__/__

WEDNESDAY __/__/__

THURSDAY __/__/__

FRIDAY __/__/__

SATURDAY __/__/__   SUNDAY __/__/__

MONDAY __/__/__

TUESDAY __/__/__

WEDNESDAY __/__/__

THURSDAY __/__/__

FRIDAY __/__/__

SATURDAY __/__/__   SUNDAY __/__/__

WEEK 13

☆ Write about your *favorite* things.

What is your favorite color?

Your favorite food?

Your favorite holiday?

Your favorite song?

Your favorite game?

Your favorite sport?

Your favorite season?

Your favorite movie?

Your favorite animal?

Your favorite ice cream?

Your favorite, favorite anything?

WEEK 14

☆ Everyone has likes and *dislikes*. The world would be a boring place if we all had the same opinions about everything. List some of your dislikes.

What food do you dislike the most?

Is there a song that you feverishly dislike?

What color do you dislike more than anything?

Is there a specific place you dislike?

What kind of weather do you dislike?

What store do you dislike going to?

What random thing do you really, really, really dislike?

MONDAY __/__/__

TUESDAY __/__/__

WEDNESDAY __/__/__

THURSDAY __/__/__

FRIDAY __/__/__

SATURDAY __/__/__

SUNDAY __/__/__

MONDAY __/__/__

TUESDAY __/__/__

WEDNESDAY __/__/__

THURSDAY __/__/__

FRIDAY __/__/__

SATURDAY __/__/__

SUNDAY __/__/__

WEEK 15

☆ You wrote your *likes* and *dislikes* over the last 2 weeks. Now it's story time.
Write about a character who likes your dislikes, and dislikes your likes.

_____

_____

_____

_____

_____

_____

_____

_____

_____

WEEK 16

☆ Would you rather wake up to find that you're 5 years *younger* or 5 years *older*?

☆ Give three reasons for your answer.

Journal or Schedule Important Moments from your Week

MONDAY __/__/__

TUESDAY __/__/__

WEDNESDAY __/__/__

THURSDAY __/__/__

FRIDAY __/__/__

SATURDAY __/__/__

SUNDAY __/__/__

MONDAY __/__/__

TUESDAY __/__/__

WEDNESDAY __/__/__

THURSDAY __/__/__

FRIDAY __/__/__

SATURDAY __/__/__

SUNDAY __/__/__

WEEK 17

☆ What is your *talent*?

☆ What 3 things would you like to *learn* how to do and what would you do with those abilities?

☆ Some kids know what they want to be when they *grow up*, and some aren't sure. Which one are you?

☆ If you know what you want to be when you grow up, write a paragraph describing your day as that person. If you don't know what you want to be yet, invent a *new* type of career or industry that doesn't exist, and write a paragraph about what it's like to have that job.

_____

_____

_____

_____

_____

_____

_____

_____

_____

MONDAY __/__/__

TUESDAY __/__/__

WEDNESDAY __/__/__

THURSDAY __/__/__

FRIDAY __/__/__

SATURDAY __/__/__

SUNDAY __/__/__

MONDAY __/__/__

TUESDAY __/__/__

WEDNESDAY __/__/__

THURSDAY __/__/__

FRIDAY __/__/__

SATURDAY __/__/__

SUNDAY __/__/__

WEEK 19

☆ What is your biggest *fear*?

☆ What is the *scariest* thing that's ever happened to you?

☆ What is something people are *afraid* of that you aren't?

☆ What's your favorite *scary movie*?

☆ What's the name of the creature looking in through *your* window?

☆ Did that last question make you look?

WEEK 20

☆ Write a list of at least 12 things that put you in a *good mood*.

_____

_____

_____

_____

_____

_____

_____

_____

_____

_____

_____

Journal or Schedule Important Moments from your Week

MONDAY __/__/__

TUESDAY __/__/__

WEDNESDAY __/__/__

THURSDAY __/__/__

FRIDAY __/__/__

SATURDAY __/__/__

SUNDAY __/__/__

MONDAY __/__/__

TUESDAY __/__/__

WEDNESDAY __/__/__

THURSDAY __/__/__

FRIDAY __/__/__

SATURDAY __/__/__

SUNDAY __/__/__

WEEK 21

☆ Do you ever wonder if there is life on other planets? *Imagine* you are living 500 years in the future and all humanity lives in a giant city floating in space. How would we travel from place to place?

☆ What would our *houses* be like?

☆ What would we *eat*?

☆ What kind of *pets* would we have?

☆ What do you think it would be like to live without *weather*?

☆ What would kids do for *fun*?

WEEK 22

☆ Imagine everyone in your family has their own *unique* super power or magical ability. Write about which family member has which ability and what they mostly use them for.

_____

_____

_____

_____

_____

_____

_____

_____

_____

Journal or Schedule Important Moments from your Week

MONDAY __/__/__

TUESDAY __/__/__

WEDNESDAY __/__/__

THURSDAY __/__/__

FRIDAY __/__/__

SATURDAY __/__/__

SUNDAY __/__/__

MONDAY __/__/__

TUESDAY __/__/__

WEDNESDAY __/__/__

THURSDAY __/__/__

FRIDAY __/__/__

SATURDAY __/__/__

SUNDAY __/__/__

WEEK 23

☆ Finish the *story* using only words that start with V, Z, T and P. You must use each letter at least once and no more than 4 times. Don't use the same word more than once.

Once upon a dark stormy night, a _____

was traveling from _____ when suddenly a _____

fell from the sky a landed on the _____. Everyone was

shocked except for _____ who was too busy eating _____.

Then without warning, a large _____ came roaring by

and made everyone _____ until they couldn't stand it

anymore. So they all gathered their _____ and decided to

head for _____ to see the mysterious stranger who

promised everyone would get all the _____ they could

ever want. It was a wonderful occasion, and everyone celebrated with lots of

_____ and _____. They they all

fell asleep in the _____ and snored happily ever after.

WEEK 24

☆ List your 5 *favorite* foods, and 5 foods you won't dare eat.

_____

_____

_____

_____

_____

_____

_____

_____

_____

MONDAY __/__/__

TUESDAY __/__/__

WEDNESDAY __/__/__

THURSDAY __/__/__

FRIDAY __/__/__

SATURDAY __/__/__

SUNDAY __/__/__

Journal or Schedule Important Moments from your Week

MONDAY __/__/__

TUESDAY __/__/__

WEDNESDAY __/__/__

THURSDAY __/__/__

FRIDAY __/__/__

SATURDAY __/__/__

SUNDAY __/__/__

☆ You have been given 3 *wishes*. What are they, and what will you do with them?

_____

_____

_____

_____

_____

_____

_____

_____

_____

_____

_____

WEEK 26

☆ You've been given a choice, to be able to speak *every language* on earth, or speak to *every animal* on earth. Which do you choose and what do you do with your amazing gift?

_____

_____

_____

_____

_____

_____

_____

_____

_____

MONDAY __/__/__

TUESDAY __/__/__

WEDNESDAY __/__/__

THURSDAY __/__/__

FRIDAY __/__/__

SATURDAY __/__/__

SUNDAY __/__/__

MONDAY __/__/__

TUESDAY __/__/__

WEDNESDAY __/__/__

THURSDAY __/__/__

FRIDAY __/__/__

SATURDAY __/__/__

SUNDAY __/__/__

WEEK 27

☆ You have been awarded one trip through time. Would you rather go back in time to meet your *ancestors* or go into the future to meet your *grandchildren?*

☆ Make a list of 5 *questions* you would ask them.

_____

_____

_____

_____

_____

_____

_____

_____

WEEK 28

☆ Positive *affirmations* help to build a healthy mindset and positive self esteem. Finish the sentences below with your own words and use them when you are feeling down.

I am _____

I can _____

I believe in _____

I'm grateful for _____

I love _____

I will _____

I know _____

Journal or Schedule Important Moments from your Week

MONDAY __/__/__

TUESDAY __/__/__

WEDNESDAY __/__/__

THURSDAY __/__/__

FRIDAY __/__/__

SATURDAY __/__/__

SUNDAY __/__/__

MONDAY __/__/__

TUESDAY __/__/__

WEDNESDAY __/__/__

THURSDAY __/__/__

FRIDAY __/__/__

SATURDAY __/__/__

SUNDAY __/__/__

WEEK 29

☆ If you could be *any animal* you like (real or fantasy) for one day, which would you choose, and why?

WEEK 30

☆ What would you do if you woke up one morning to find yourself *invisible*? Would you prank people or help people? Write a story about what your unusual experience might be like.

_____

_____

_____

_____

_____

_____

_____

_____

_____

Journal or Schedule Important Moments from your Week

MONDAY __/__/__

TUESDAY __/__/__

WEDNESDAY __/__/__

THURSDAY __/__/__

FRIDAY __/__/__

SATURDAY __/__/__

SUNDAY __/__/__

MONDAY __/__/__

TUESDAY __/__/__

WEDNESDAY __/__/__

THURSDAY __/__/__

FRIDAY __/__/__

SATURDAY __/__/__

SUNDAY __/__/__

WEEK 31

☆ The thing I wish other people would *understand* about me is…

_____

_____

_____

_____

_____

_____

_____

_____

_____

_____

WEEK 32

☆ Draw your *family tree* as far back as you can.

Journal or Schedule Important Moments from your Week

MONDAY __/__/__

TUESDAY __/__/__

WEDNESDAY __/__/__

THURSDAY __/__/__

FRIDAY __/__/__

SATURDAY __/__/__

SUNDAY __/__/__

MONDAY __/__/__

TUESDAY __/__/__

WEDNESDAY __/__/__

THURSDAY __/__/__

FRIDAY __/__/__

SATURDAY __/__/__

SUNDAY __/__/__

WEEK 33

☆ Finish the *story* using only words that start with G, J, D and B. You must use each letter at least once and no more than 4 times. Don't use the same word more than once.

It was raining cats and _____. The road ahead was blocked

by a large _____, so my _____ took me to

the _____ instead where we found shelter and food. We

ate lots of _____ and slept on _____.

The next morning to our surprise, there was a bunch of _____

heading for woods, where we all saw a _____ in the sky. I

took a picture and later that day the news showed my picture to the whole

_____ making me famous overnight. I was then made

the ambassador of _____ and moved to

_____ to live out the rest of my life. But my big secret is I

kept the _____ I found that day and never told

another soul until now.

WEEK 34

☆ Write your 5 favorite *songs*, and one song you hope you never have to hear again.

Journal or Schedule Important Moments from your Week

MONDAY __/__/__

TUESDAY __/__/__

WEDNESDAY __/__/__

THURSDAY __/__/__

FRIDAY __/__/__

SATURDAY __/__/__   SUNDAY __/__/__

MONDAY __/__/__

TUESDAY __/__/__

WEDNESDAY __/__/__

THURSDAY __/__/__

FRIDAY __/__/__

SATURDAY __/__/__

SUNDAY __/__/__

WEEK 35

☆ When you grow up, what do you think will be the childhood memories you'll most want to remember?

_____

_____

_____

_____

_____

_____

_____

_____

_____

WEEK 36

☆ Let's talk about *school life*. What is your favorite subject?

☆ What subject are you *best* at?

☆ What subject are you *worst* at?

☆ How can you *improve* your worst subject?

☆ What do you *wish* you could learn about in school?

☆ What do you wish you *didn't* have to learn about in school?

☆ What would you most like to *change* about school?

Journal or Schedule Important Moments from your Week

MONDAY __/__/__

TUESDAY __/__/__

WEDNESDAY __/__/__

THURSDAY __/__/__

FRIDAY __/__/__

SATURDAY __/__/__

SUNDAY __/__/__

MONDAY __/__/__

TUESDAY __/__/__

WEDNESDAY __/__/__

THURSDAY __/__/__

FRIDAY __/__/__

SATURDAY __/__/__

SUNDAY __/__/__

WEEK 37

☆ What is the **strangest dream** you've ever had? What do you *think* your dream was telling you?

_____

_____

_____

_____

_____

_____

_____

_____

_____

_____

WEEK 38

☆ Design and draw a *trendy outfit* that you think kids your age will be wearing 100 years from now.

Journal or Schedule Important Moments from your Week

MONDAY __/__/__

TUESDAY __/__/__

WEDNESDAY __/__/__

THURSDAY __/__/__

FRIDAY __/__/__

SATURDAY __/__/__

SUNDAY __/__/__

MONDAY __/__/__

TUESDAY __/__/__

WEDNESDAY __/__/__

THURSDAY __/__/__

FRIDAY __/__/__

SATURDAY __/__/__

SUNDAY __/__/__

WEEK 39

☆ You've just been chosen as the new **Queen** of your country and have been given absolute authority to change or create any new laws. What are the first 5 things you would do to make your country better for the people?

WEEK 40

☆ You woke up to find yourself in *another* decade within the last 100 years. What decade is it, and what is the first thing you do while exploring that era?

_____

_____

_____

_____

_____

_____

_____

_____

_____

_____

Journal or Schedule Important Moments from your Week

MONDAY __/__/__

TUESDAY __/__/__

WEDNESDAY __/__/__

THURSDAY __/__/__

FRIDAY __/__/__

SATURDAY __/__/__

SUNDAY __/__/__

MONDAY __/__/__

TUESDAY __/__/__

WEDNESDAY __/__/__

THURSDAY __/__/__

FRIDAY __/__/__

SATURDAY __/__/__

SUNDAY __/__/__

WEEK 41

☆ Make a list of 10 things that help you to *relax*. The next time you are feeling stressed, come back to this list and give it a try.

_____

_____

_____

_____

_____

_____

_____

_____

WEEK 42

☆ Create a *vision board* on this page. You can use cut out pictures or draw your own. Your vision board can have any goals or wishes you want to achieve in this lifetime.

MONDAY __/__/__

TUESDAY __/__/__

WEDNESDAY __/__/__

THURSDAY __/__/__

FRIDAY __/__/__

SATURDAY __/__/__

SUNDAY __/__/__

MONDAY __/__/__

TUESDAY __/__/__

WEDNESDAY __/__/__

THURSDAY __/__/__

FRIDAY __/__/__

SATURDAY __/__/__

SUNDAY __/__/__

WEEK 43

☆ In what ways have you *changed* in the last year? Write 3 examples.

_____

_____

_____

_____

_____

_____

_____

_____

_____

_____

WEEK 44

☆ Have you ever had a close friend or family member *move* far away? Write down what that experience was like for you. If you have not, write down how you would feel if your closest friend or family member had to move.

_____

_____

_____

_____

_____

_____

_____

_____

_____

_____

Journal or Schedule Important Moments from your Week

MONDAY __/__/__

TUESDAY __/__/__

WEDNESDAY __/__/__

THURSDAY __/__/__

FRIDAY __/__/__

SATURDAY __/__/__

SUNDAY __/__/__

MONDAY __/__/__

TUESDAY __/__/__

WEDNESDAY __/__/__

THURSDAY __/__/__

FRIDAY __/__/__

SATURDAY __/__/__

SUNDAY __/__/__

WEEK 45

☆ Write a *different ending* to one of your favorite movies.

WEEK 46

☆ Do you think people should marry for *love* or for *money*? Write about the advantages and disadvantages of each option,.

_____

_____

_____

_____

_____

_____

_____

_____

_____

_____

Journal or Schedule Important Moments from your Week

MONDAY __/__/__

TUESDAY __/__/__

WEDNESDAY __/__/__

THURSDAY __/__/__

FRIDAY __/__/__

SATURDAY __/__/__

SUNDAY __/__/__

MONDAY __/__/__

TUESDAY __/__/__

WEDNESDAY __/__/__

THURSDAY __/__/__

FRIDAY __/__/__

SATURDAY __/__/__

SUNDAY __/__/__

WEEK 47

☆ Write a letter to your *great-great grandmother* and tell her all about yourself, your parents, and grandparents. Tell her about the world today and how much it's changed since she was alive. You can write the letter on a separate paper or stationary, and put it between these pages for safe keeping.

Dearest Great-Great Grandmother...........

WEEK 48

☆ Think of an event that *changed* your life forever. Imagine instead a different outcome to that event, and write down how different your life would be today.

_____

_____

_____

_____

_____

_____

_____

_____

_____

_____

_____

Journal or Schedule Important Moments from your Week

MONDAY __/__/__

TUESDAY __/__/__

WEDNESDAY __/__/__

THURSDAY __/__/__

FRIDAY __/__/__

SATURDAY __/__/__

SUNDAY __/__/__

MONDAY __/__/__

TUESDAY __/__/__

WEDNESDAY __/__/__

THURSDAY __/__/__

FRIDAY __/__/__

SATURDAY __/__/__

SUNDAY __/__/__

WEEK 49

☆ Write about your favorite birthday. How old were you? What made it so special?

_____

_____

_____

_____

_____

_____

_____

_____

_____

_____

WEEK 50

☆ What one object from childhood will you keep with you through adulthood, and why?

_____

_____

_____

_____

_____

_____

_____

_____

_____

_____

Journal or Schedule Important Moments from your Week

MONDAY __/__/__

TUESDAY __/__/__

WEDNESDAY __/__/__

THURSDAY __/__/__

FRIDAY __/__/__

SATURDAY __/__/__

SUNDAY __/__/__

Journal or Schedule Important Moments from your Week

MONDAY __/__/__

TUESDAY __/__/__

WEDNESDAY __/__/__

THURSDAY __/__/__

FRIDAY __/__/__

SATURDAY __/__/__

SUNDAY __/__/__

WEEK 51

☆ Who do you most look up to and why?

_____

_____

_____

_____

_____

_____

_____

_____

_____

_____

_____

WEEK 52

☆ Congratulations! You've just completed ONE YEAR of journaling, self discovery, imaginative thinking, and creative expression. Did you compete the goal you wrote about on week one? Why or why not? What have you learned about yourself this year? Will you keep a journal for next year?

_____

_____

_____

_____

_____

_____

_____

_____

_____

_____

Journal or Schedule Important Moments from your Week

MONDAY __/__/__

TUESDAY __/__/__

WEDNESDAY __/__/__

THURSDAY __/__/__

FRIDAY __/__/__

SATURDAY __/__/__   SUNDAY __/__/__

Printed in Great Britain
by Amazon